The Master's Touch

Illustration Credits

The Eleventh at Augusta, *Isaiah 40:8*
20" x 30", Oil
Pages 32-33, 48 & cover

Pebble Beach, *Psalm 96:11*
17" x 34", Oil
Pages 16 & 18-19

The Sixteenth at Barton Creek, *Psalm 107:35*
30" x 36", Oil
Pages 24-25 & 41

The Thirteenth at the Atlanta Country Club,
Psalm 121:5
20" x 24", Oil
Pages 22 & 45

The Thirteenth at Valhalla, *Psalm 116:7*
20" x 30", Oil
Page 8

"Birds" at Seven, *Isaiah 51:15*
24" x 36", Oil
Pages 34-35

Number One at the Boulders, *Psalm 18:2*
22" x 44", Oil
Pages 36 & 38-39

The Seventeenth at Shoal Creek, *Deuteronomy 8:7*
22" x 44", Oil
Pages 14-15

The Thirteenth at Kauai Lagoon, *Psalm 69:34*
12" x 9", Oil
Page 30

The Fifteenth at Cypress Point, *Psalm 93:4*
30" x 60", Oil
Pages 7, 29 & back cover

Take Time, *Philippians 4:8*
28" x 22", Oil
Pages 10 & 43

Golf's Greatest Corner I, The 11th, *Psalm 40:4*
9" x 12", Oil
Page 5

Golf's Greatest Corner II, The 12th, *Psalm 40:4*
9" x 12", Oil
Page 21

Golf's Greatest Corner III, The 13th, *Psalm 40:4*
12" x 9", Oil
Page 26

The 12th at La Cantera, *Isaiah 48:21*
12" x 9", Oil
Page 13

The Master's Touch

PAINTINGS BY LARRY DYKE

WRITTEN BY TED SPRAGUE

Credits and Acknowledgements:

Paintings Copyright © 2000 Larry Dyke
Somerset House Publishing, Inc.,
Houston, Texas

Text Copyright © 2000 Ted Sprague

All rights reserved

Printed in Belgium

Published by Broadman & Holman Publishers, Nashville, Tennessee
www.broadmanholman.com
Cover and interior design by Paul T. Gant, Art & Design, Nashville, Tennessee

ISBN 0-8054-3534-4

Scriptures taken from the HOLY BIBLE, NEW INTERNATIONAL VERSION
Copyright © 1973, 1978, 1984 International Bible Society
Used by permission of Zondervan Bible Publishers

Larry Dyke's signed, limited edition
golf prints and canvases are available from
Somerset House Publishing, Inc.
Call 1-800-444-2540
or log on at www.somersethouse.com

First Hole

INTRODUCTION

The Master's Touch respectfully acknowledges some of the greatest golfers of the century:

Jack Nicklaus, Bobby Jones, Ben Hogan, Sam Snead, Arnold Palmer, Byron Nelson, Harry Vardon, Gary Player, Walter Hagen, Gene Sarazen, Tiger Woods

These and many other top professional men and women golfers have captivated spectators worldwide with their skill and accomplishment as they have challenged magnificent golf courses and breathtaking holes. These extraordinary people possess a master's touch.

Larry Dyke has painted some of the most inspiring holes in golf. This book contains several of his paintings depicting the character, challenge, and natural terrain of some of the very best holes in golf. He has the master's touch in making these spectacular scenes come alive.

This book is dedicated to the memory of Payne Stewart, whose life and legacy exemplifies the true Master's touch.

ISAIAH 40:7,8

Second Hole

GOLF AND LIFE ... SO MUCH IN COMMON

They both can be so satisfying and likewise so frustrating ...
both are definitely CHALLENGING.
Men and women face critical challenges in life including:

*loss of health, broken relationships, financial stress,
addictions, corporate politics, loneliness,
loss of job, strife, restlessness, loss of love,
peer pressure, character flaws, loss of hope, and
countless other challenges and pressures of life.*

We need the Master's touch to face each day.

*In addition, we need to be encouraged by the Master's touch to
see the big picture whether we are at the golf course, at work,
in the neighborhood, or wherever we interact with people.*

A TRUE STORY: THE ARKANSAS GOLFER

What would you say if you were asked by the widow of a man you played golf with weekly for 7 years, to say something on behalf of your deceased golfing buddy? A man was asked that question, and the next day he phoned the wife and told her he really did not know what to say. She asked the man what they talked about while playing golf? "Only golf", he replied.

How sad if that is also true of us on the golf course, or in our daily lives. The purpose of these writings is to encourage people to develop the master's touch in golf and the Master's touch with people. We should live out our faith daily in our own lives and in the lives of others.

PSALM 93:4

Third Hole

THE MASTER'S TOUCH IN GOLF AND LIFE

Recognized as the greatest shot in golf competition, Gene Sarazen won the Masters in 1935, when he holed a four wood for a double eagle on the 15th at Augusta National during the Masters Golf Tournament. The greatest string of victories—Byron Nelson in 1945 when he won 11 straight PGA tour wins. The king—Arnold Palmer with his unforgettable charisma and his countless great performances. He alone is responsible for the tremendous popularity of golf. The greatest—Jack Nicklaus, acknowledged as one of the most outstanding golfers of all time.

As amateurs we know only too well that truly good shots are rare, because most of us deal with bad shots, three putts, and a lack of timing and balance. However, even the pros have tough times.

That is why golf is so challenging for those who play the game. Many people play it for relaxation, exercise, companionship, accomplishment, and competition. Some people play the game just to get away from the normal routine of life.

Grantland Rice, a famous journalist of the Bobby Jones era said it best, "Golf is 20% mechanics and technique. The other 80% is philosophy, humor, tragedy, romance, melodrama, companionship, comradery, cursedness, and conversation."

Stop and think about all that goes into a golf swing—grip, stance, balance, timing, and follow-through. Much more goes into developing our faith.

The Lord wants to add to our faith, additional qualities such as goodness, knowledge, self-control, perseverance, godliness, brotherly kindness, and love.

"For if you possess these qualities in increasing measure, they will keep you from being ineffective and unproductive in your knowledge of our Lord Jesus Christ."

2 Peter 1:8

We can get a glimpse of God's insight on how to approach life by comparing golf and life, and looking at the unique challenges each represents.

Fourth Hole

ONE STROKE & ONE DAY AT A TIME

GOLF INSIGHT

"It is nothing new or original to say that golf is played one stroke at a time. But it took me years to realize it."

Bobby Jones

GOD'S INSIGHT

"Therefore do not worry about tomorrow, for tomorrow will worry about itself. Each day has enough trouble of its own."

Matthew 6:34

After a double bogey, due to hitting the ball out of bounds, it is very hard not to be discouraged. Tiger Woods, during a prestigious international tournament, hit an excellent shot over water on hole number 17. He hit a nine-iron directly into a stiff wind, and the ball landed about ten feet beyond the hole only to back up past the hole and roll ever so slowly into the water. He took an 8 on that hole. The next hole he kept his cool and made par while he waited for his nearest competition to finish the tournament.

Tiger won the tournament in a play-off with a birdie. It would have been so easy for him to have blown his cool and let the TRIPLE BOGEY destroy his very next hole. Instead, he regained his composure and went on to par the hole and birdie the first play-off hole to win the prestigious international tournament. Why? Because he played the game one shot at a time.

Similarly, living a day at a time in the midst of problems can sometimes be a challenge. Additionally, financial pressures, addictions, communication breakdowns and countless other realities of life can be very grueling and difficult. However, God tells us in His Word to live one day at a time, because each day has enough trouble of its own.

Through God's strength, and by claiming His promises, we can live one day at a time. Is God saying not to plan ahead? Absolutely not. What He is saying, is in times of excruciating trials we must focus on living one day at a time.

One of the secrets to playing better golf is to concentrate on playing one stroke at a time, and one of the secrets to contentment in the midst of pain is to insist on living within the day, focused on the promises of God.

It is one thing to read God's promises and yet it is another thing to apply them to our lives.

Fifth Hole

WE ALL CHOKE

GOLF INSIGHT

"We all choke. You are not human if you haven't."

Curtis Strange

GOD'S INSIGHT

"For all have sinned and fall short of the glory of God, and are justified freely by his grace through the redemption that came by Christ Jesus."

Romans 3:23-24

GOLF & LIFE

In their December 1999 issue, *Golf* magazine ran an article about some of the worst chokes in the history of golf. Ken Venturi attempted to become the only amateur to ever win the Masters. He shot a closing day 80, to lose by one stroke. At the 1970 British Open, Doug Sanders, missed a putt from three feet on the final hole, which put him into a play-off. He lost the play-off to Jack Nicklaus.

Amateur golfers understand very well what it means to miss on a short putt. Having played a par 4, par 5, or even a tough par 3, and being on the green in regulation only to three-putt from a short distance is truly exasperating.

We all know what it is like to choke and do something we should not have done. God tells us that we all have sinned and fallen short of His glory. We are imperfect. If we were perfect, there would be no reason for His redemptive grace through his son Jesus Christ.

Dear God,
We've all "choked." When I sin, help me to know Your forgiveness and love through Christ. Help me to grow spiritually, so that I will not only believe in grace, but be known as a gracious person. Let the fruit of Your Spirit abound in my life.

Sixth Hole

GOLF IS A GAME OF HONOR

GOLF INSIGHT

"It's just good sportsmanship not to pick up the ball while it is still rolling."

Mark Twain

GOD'S INSIGHT

"Who can discern his errors? Forgive my hidden faults. Keep your servant also from willful sins; may they not rule over me."

Psalm 19:12-13

President George Bush said, "Golf is unique in the values it teaches. A game of honor, integrity and good sportsmanship, golf is governed by the players themselves, who by sticking to the spirit and discipline of the game, gain the personal fulfillment of pride, self-esteem and self-discipline."

GOLF & LIFE

Mark Twain's joke about not picking up a ball while it is still rolling, although funny, applies to golfers. Golf is a game of honor and cheating is not allowed. God is very aware of our actions. In Psalm 19:14 it says, "May the words of my mouth and the meditation of my heart be pleasing in your sight, O LORD, my Rock and my Redeemer." Obviously, we as Christians should have very high moral standards, and we should never be accused of cheating. However, when we do fail because of sin, we need to confess and repent of our sins. Confession and repentance is healthy for our souls.

Dear Father,
Help me to never be accused of knowingly cheating. In all of life, help me to live above reproach. When I do fail, help me to realize that is why Christ came—because I couldn't keep the law, and I need Your grace.

Seventh Hole

HUNTING & FISHING

GOLF INSIGHT

"The only reason I played golf was so I could afford to go hunting & fishing."

Sam Snead

GOD'S INSIGHT

"As Jesus walked beside the Sea of Galilee, he saw Simon and his brother Andrew casting a net into the lake, for they were fishermen. 'Come, follow me,' Jesus said, 'and I will make you fishers of men.'"

Mark 1:16-17

GOLF & LIFE

Sam Snead's comments about enjoying other areas of life certainly catches our attention. When we get to heaven, God will not ask us about our handicap.

Lee Trevino jokingly said, "I'm a golfaholic and all the counseling in the world won't help me." To those of us who love the game of golf, we talk about it, we wake up thinking about it, we watch golf on television or in person, and of course, we all love to play the game. Is there any doubt that we have four or five hours during a round of golf to proclaim God's love as part of our conversation with others?

God reminds us that the Son of Man came to seek and to save that which is lost (Luke 19:10). He will ask us about the people we golfed with, and if we were a part of the process of introducing others to Christ. God wants us to be "golfers of men" as we play, but very few Christians witness on the golf course for fear of rejection or disapproval. Many do not want to risk the loss of friendship by discussing the gospel.

Additionally, some Christian golfers who try to witness, do it in a negative and harsh way. Such persons generally fail to take the time to genuinely love, and gently introduce other golfers to the gospel—the good news of Jesus Christ. Such witnessing becomes "hit and run" rather than devoting oneself to establishing a relationship with another person. How exciting it would be if we not only enjoyed the game of golf, but used golf and our passion for the game to create a safe environment in which we could share our faith.

If we would pray these verses before and during every round ...

"Devote yourselves to prayer, being watchful and thankful. And pray for us, too, that God may open a door for our message, so that we may proclaim the mystery of Christ, for which I am in chains.

Pray that I may proclaim it clearly, as I should. Be wise in the way you act toward outsiders; make the most of every opportunity. Let your conversation always be full of grace, seasoned with salt, so that you may know how to answer everyone."

Colossians 4:2-6

Sharing God's love is more rewarding than an eagle on the back nine. God wants us to enjoy a wonderful game of golf and the fulfillment it brings, but He also wants us to never forget how important the people we play golf with are. Our purpose in life is to share the good news of God's love and grace with people who desperately need peace with God more than pars.

Lord, I not only want to be a friend to my golfing partners, but to share by word and example the "best news in life". Help me to be an encouraging and supportive friend in times of need, and to focus on building relationships with those You place within my reach.

Eighth Hole

BALANCE ... THE SECRET TO GOLF AND LIFE

GOLF INSIGHT

When three pros, who have all won tournaments, were recently questioned, "What is the most important aspect of a golf swing?" They each independently replied, "balance."

GOD'S INSIGHT

"And what does the LORD require of you? To act justly and to love mercy and to walk humbly with your God."

Micah 6:8

Most amateur golfers are so unbalanced. Whether you are watching golf on television or in person, it is always amazing to see the perfect balance that professional golfers maintain while swinging a golf club. Balance is the distinctive between a single digit handicap and a double digit handicap. Balance plays an important role in hitting a proper golf shot.

In golf, as in life, we need balance. So many times our lives become unbalanced. We choose activities over being involved in the lives of others. We trade the urgent for the important things in life. It is important that we maintain a balance of love, justice, mercy, and humility.

God's Word challenges us to try and maintain a balanced reputation as we live our lives with others.

Think about the characteristics of the most balanced people you know, then think about how your reputation and character looks to others. Are you known only as a person of justice? Do you stand up for what is right and wrong, see things as simply black and white? If so, then perhaps you lack mercy. Are you known only as a person of mercy—one who is concerned about other people, and is willing to give them a second chance, and the benefit of the doubt as long as they are sincere? Then perhaps you lack justice.

God wants us to balance ... love, justice, mercy and humility in our lives.

ISAIAH 40:7-8

If we want to be better golfers, we need to learn from the pros the importance of balance in a golf swing. If we want to lead a more balanced life, we need to ask God for wisdom and discernment.

Dear God,
By Your mercy and grace,
help me to balance justice
with mercy, and walk humbly
with You. Help me to be aware
of how admirable it is to be
a balanced person, and sense
a greater leading of the
Holy Spirit in my life.

Ninth Hole

FULFILLMENT

GOLF INSIGHT

"There are no absolutes in golf. Golf is such an individual game, and no two people swing alike."

Kathy Whitworth

GOD'S INSIGHT

"Now the body is not made up of one part but of many."

I Corinthians 12:14

GOLF & LIFE

Most people agree that Arnold Palmer is the most charismatic golfer that has ever lived. In his prime, his golf swing and demeanor were electrifying and captivating. Most amateurs who try to imitate his swing fail miserably because his approach was so different from the normal textbook golf swing. Arnie's results were extraordinary. He is perhaps the most popular golfer of all time, and his achievements are remarkable. He won the Masters, the U.S. Open, the British Open, and dozens of other tournaments through the years.

Like golf swings, spiritual gifts are also different. In the Bible, I Corinthians 12, Romans 12, and Ephesians 4, talk about how we are all gifted in different ways. In many of these verses, God compares us to parts of the body. Not everyone has the same function. Not everyone has the same giftedness.

We all need each other, because that's the way God made us. Insight requires that we discover our spiritual giftedness and then exercise that gift. God does not make inferior people. Everyone plays a part in God's kingdom. We should not try to be somebody else, but we should seek to become the person whom God made us to be. Each of us have at least one spiritual gift, and we need to exercise that gift to build up the body of Christ and to serve our Lord and Savior Jesus Christ.

"The eye cannot say to the hand, 'I don't need you.'"

I Corinthians 12:21

Dear Lord,
Help me to accept my uniqueness and giftedness. Help me to use my gifts to build up others in their faith, and by doing so, find peace and fulfillment in my own life.

Tenth Hole

ADVERSITY & SUFFERING

GOLF INSIGHT

"Adversity is the fork in the road. You'll get better or you'll get worse, but you'll never stay the same."

Ken Venturi

GOD'S INSIGHT

"Not only so, but we also rejoice in our sufferings, because we know that suffering produces perseverance; perseverance, character; and character, hope. And hope does not disappoint us, because God has poured out his love into our hearts by the Holy Spirit, whom he has given us."

Romans 5:3-5

Dear Lord,
Help me be transformed when I face adversity.
When golf is bad, help me to keep the game in its
proper perspective. In life, help me know that trials
and adversity give me an opportunity to trust more
in You and less in myself. In times of distress,
Your commands are my delight. In the day of
trouble, I call out to You, and You save me.

GOLF & LIFE

Recently, an attorney who is an avid golfer with an 18 handicap, said after 45 holes of playing poorly that he finally discovered what he was doing wrong. It was a small adjustment, but that small adjustment allowed him to turn his game completely around. This also holds true for professionals. Larry Nelson, at one point in his life before he won three major tournaments, was ready to give up the game of golf. Then someone showed him a little thing he was doing wrong with his arm.

Not too very long ago, Doug Sanders, the flamboyant dresser and outstanding golfer, encountered a serious health situation in his life. A debilitating disease almost killed him, and during that time of facing death he asked God to come into his life, and specifically asked Jesus Christ to be his Savior. This seemingly small adjustment changed his life.

For us, the challenge may come in the loss of a job, loss of our health, or various other difficulties. These represent forks in the road, and it is here that we need to concentrate on how God, through His Holy Spirit can give us the strength of character that we cannot possibly gain during the good times. As God's Word says, we can rejoice in our sufferings because they can actually produce perseverance in our lives, develop character, and create a hope that is centered on God. In tough times we need to put our faith in Jesus Christ.

ISAIAH 40:7 & 8

Eleventh Hole

ATTEMPTING THE DRAMATIC

GOLF INSIGHT

"It has been my experience, since a kid going to play, that if you try to sink a chip shot you will get closer to the hole. And occasionally make one."

Tom Watson

GOD'S INSIGHT

"Sow your seed in the morning, and at evening let not your hands be idle, for you do not know which will succeed, whether this or that, or whether both will do equally well."

Ecclesiastes 11:6

GOLF & LIFE

Watching the pros make miraculous shots that amateurs can only dream of, is inspiring. Occasionally, we will make shots that are more luck than skill. Tom Watson recommends the amateur think in terms of making the shot which allows the ball to get closer to the hole, and perhaps on occasion, it will go in.

In life, if we are looking for a job it is important to have several interviews, because "hot leads" can turn cold, and those leads that appear hopeless can suddenly bear fruit. This also applies to making sales calls, proposals or business plans. We've all heard the saying, "Don't put all of your eggs in one basket."

The same thing holds true when it comes to sharing our faith with others. God's Word is very clear—in I Corinthians 3:5-9, the apostle Paul illustrates how we are a part of a larger process.

Paul says that we all play a part in sharing the gospel, but God is the key player. It is important to realize that we never know how or where our seed (influence) may fall. Some will fall on fertile ground and will produce fruit, while others will fall on rocky ground and wash away. Our job is simply to be part of the process of planting the gospel in people's lives through grace, humility and mercy.

Dear Lord,
Help me to be a faithful planter and leave the results to You. I don't know where or when the seed I plant will produce fruit. I need to acknowledge You and sow faithfully, whether I am looking for a job or sharing the best news in life, may I leave the results in Your loving hands.

Twelfth Hole

PRESSURE
WHAT SCORE DO WE HAVE TO SHOOT TO GET INTO HEAVEN?

GOLF INSIGHT

The pressure makes me more intent about each shot. Pressure on the last few holes makes me play better.

Nancy Lopez

GOD'S INSIGHT

For it is by the grace you have been saved, through faith—and this not from yourselves, it is the gift of God—not by works, so that no one can boast."

Ephesians 2: 8-9

GOLF & LIFE

There are many sports in which a "perfect" game or score is attainable. You can bowl a perfect game. You can score a perfect "ten" in gymnastics and figure skating. You can even pitch a perfect game in baseball. However, it's impossible to shoot a perfect game of golf. A par 72 for the course isn't perfect because it is possible to shoot below par on every hole. In order to shoot a perfect score for one round, it would require a score of 18. Not only is that a lot of pressure to try and put on someone, it is impossible to do. It's also impossible to live a "perfect" life in word, thought, and deed. Yet, many people believe that we have to be "perfect" in order to earn our way to heaven.

Let's look at the Ten Commandments that God gave to Moses on Mount Sinai:

You shall have no other gods before me.
You shall not make for yourself an idol.
You shall not misuse the name of the Lord your God.
Remember the Sabbath day by keeping it Holy.
Honor your father and your mother.
You shall not murder.
You shall not commit adultery.
You shall not steal.
You shall not give false testimony.
You shall not covet.

Exodus 20:3-17

By thought, word and deed we've broken the Ten Commandments hundreds of times! If we have to be perfect to get into heaven, then who can? Only those who are recipients of the grace of God, through Christ.

Pray for the Protection of Newborns!

"... I have set before you life and death, blessing and cursing; therefore **choose life**, that both you and your descendants may live; that you may love the LORD your God, that you may obey His voice, and that you may cling to Him, for **He is your life** and the length of your days...."

Deuteronomy 30:19-20 (NKJV)

Lord, help me to know that just as I cannot shoot a perfect score in golf, my life cannot be perfect either. Your forgiveness, grace and mercy has taken the pressure off me trying to live a perfect life. It is You who have delivered me, when I could not do it for myself. Now, help me to forgive myself, and others as I seek to do Your will in all things.

PSALM 93:4

Thirteenth Hole

THE COURSE MUST BE PLAYED

GOLF INSIGHT

"The more I practice, the luckier I get."

Ben Hogan

GOD'S INSIGHT

"All hard work brings a profit, but mere talk leads only to poverty."

Proverbs 14:23

PSALM 69:34

GOLF & LIFE

You can take all the lessons, watch all the videos and cable networks, read all the magazines and books, and attend all the seminars, but studying, without the ability to put what you've learned into practice is only half of the equation. Obviously, to improve our game we need to have sound instruction. Many pros will tell you that even your practice range activity should have a purpose besides simply hitting balls. However, it's unimaginable that we would spend so much time practicing and never play the course. The course must be played!

The beautiful courses painted by Larry Dyke, along with the world's multitude of golf courses should be enjoyed to the fullest. The beauty and challenge of playing different courses is thrilling, and should be approached with expectation and anticipation.

In our Christian lives the course must be played as well. We must get daily instruction by reading and listening to God's Word, praying, fellowshipping with other believers, and worshiping with fellow Christians. We should take advantage of every opportunity for spiritual growth.

Just imaging how stale golf would be if we only practiced, but never played the course. Likewise, how sad it would be if we only learned about the Christian life and didn't put our faith into practice by sharing what we have learned with others, and using our faith to face the daily challenges of life. The world desperately needs hope and guidance. It is our calling to provide that hope by putting our faith into action.

Lord, help me not to deceive myself. Compel me to play the course, and finish the race strong. Help me to realize that faith without deeds is dead, and that You have called me to action, in order to bring Your hope and peace into the lives of others.

Fourteenth Hole

CHARACTER FLAWS

GOLF INSIGHT

"Golf puts men's character on the anvil and his richest qualities—patience, poise, and restraint—to the flame."

Billy Casper

GOD'S INSIGHT

"Above all, my brothers, do not swear—not by heaven or by earth or by anything else. Let your 'Yes' be yes, and your 'No' be no, or you will be condemned."

James 5:12

"May the words of my mouth and the meditation of my heart be pleasing in your sight, O LORD, my Rock and my Redeemer."

Psalm 19:14

GOLF & LIFE

After missing a short putt to tie the hole, he swore, threw his club, and tossed his ball into the water. For the next seven holes he pouted and put a damper on the environment surrounding the other three golfers. Golf sometimes brings out the worst in us and exposes our character flaws.

Strained personal relationships, financial pressure, constant self-will, addictions, unrealistic expectations, and other forms of stress can also do the same to each of us. How we choose to deal with our stress will reveal the true nature of our character and what is in our hearts. For what goes into our hearts, comes out in our lives. Stress is merely the flame that refines us into the image of our Lord, or it renders us helpless.

Dear Lord,
It's not only the big pressures that bring out a lack of character, but the small ones too. Help me to keep my tongue from profanity and useless speech. Help me to apply Your Holy Spirit's calming influence to every missed shot and every pressure of life. Thank You for forgiving me, in the name of Jesus.

ISAIAH 51:15

Fifteenth Hole

DON'T DESTROY ... JOY

GOLF INSIGHT

"Always count your blessings. Be thankful you are able to be out on a beautiful golf course. Most people in the world don't have that opportunity."

Fred Couples

GOD'S INSIGHT

"But the fruit of the Spirit is love, joy, peace, patience, kindness, goodness, faithfulness, gentleness, and self control."

Galatians 5:22-23

GOLF & LIFE

For most of us golf should be an enjoyable recreation. Even though we try our utmost on every shot, it is not a matter of life and death. Jack Nicklaus said, "Nobody wants to win more than I do. But if I give it my best shot and fail, then life goes on. Golf, in the final analysis is only a game."

Some of us are unusually tormented by a bad round or a poor shot. When we give place to anger, our sinful nature takes over and attitudes such as hatred, discord, jealousy, fits of rage, and selfish ambition become evident.

We are called to live a life of love, joy, peace, patience, kindness, goodness, faithfulness, and self-control.

Gary Player said, "Enjoy the game. Happy golf is good golf."

Dear God,
Forgive me for sometimes not exhibiting joy on the golf course and in my life. Regardless of the kind of day I am having, help me to enjoy Your creation, and the blessings of fellowship that You have given me. Help me to get outside myself and focus on people whom You love unconditionally. Forgive me for being so self-centered, that I sometimes destroy joy. Thank You for loving me even when I am unlovable.

Sixteenth Hole

DON'T BACK YOURSELF INTO A CORNER

GOLF INSIGHT

"Everyone used to say to me, 'Glad you won the tournament.'
Now they say, 'Glad you made the cut."

Arnold Palmer

GOD'S INSIGHT

"Remember your Creator in the days of your youth, before the days of trouble come and the years approach when you will say, 'I find no pleasure in them.'"

Ecclesiastes 12:1

GOLF & LIFE

The Bible tells us our life is like a vapor. Yet many of us live as though we have all the time in the world. We will face many challenges during our lifetime. Some of us will have to deal with health issues, some perhaps terminal. Others will have to deal with the simple fact that age has its effect on us. That's why it's so important that we get our priorities right while we are young enough to have an impact.

There are young people in utter shock when their golf game and their life is interrupted due to unfortunate circumstances. They've backed themselves into a corner because they weren't realistic about life.

Whether it's a financial crisis, a job loss, health problems, or self-centeredness, we all could benefit from a proper perspective on how to handle adversity. Like hitting the ball out of the rough, our problems can provide us an opportunity to increase our skills, or we can let them render us ineffective. The best way I have found to have a balanced view of how we can live our lives to the fullest, and find grace and dignity to cope with the trials and tribulations along the way, is to spend time daily with God.

Nothing can take the place of reading God's Word. If you've never had a daily devotional time, try beginning with Psalms, Proverbs, or the book of John. Next, spend time in prayer. Pray the verses you have read for yourself and others. Finally, fellowship with other believers, sharing and encouraging one another, and get involved in a local church.

Commit your family, your relationships, and your work to the Lord, and by doing so, you will not only be able to handle the rough spots along the way, but rest assured, knowing that God is working in all things for the good of those who love Him.

Dear God,

I like to think that I have things all figured out, but the truth is, I don't. As You have said in Your Word, You allow hard times as well as prosperity so that we will realize that nothing is certain in this life, except Your love and Your grace. Help me to put priorities in order, and enjoy the life You've given me to the fullest, making the most of every day and every opportunity.

"Remember your Creator in the days of your youth, before the days of trouble come and the years approach when you will say, 'I find no pleasure in them.'"

Ecclesiastes 12:1

Seventeenth Hole

BE REALISTIC ... USE A 6-IRON

GOLF INSIGHT

"Be realistic how far you hit each club ... swinging smoothly, by not trying for maximum distance, will make you more distant consistent."

Jack Nicklaus

GOD'S INSIGHT

"For by the grace given me I say to every one of you: Do not think of yourself more highly than you ought, but rather think of yourself with sober judgment, in accordance with the measure of faith God has given you."

Romans 12:3

GOLF & LIFE

Jack Nicklaus' golf philosophy says that even though at one time we may have hit a 7-iron 160 yards, it doesn't mean we'll hit it that way every time. Nicklaus believes for every 18 holes we play, we'll hit a few perfect shots at best. Ben Hogan, a perfectionist, felt he only hit a couple of perfect shots per round. The key is to swing smoothly, and not try for more distance. At first our egos may be bruised, however, our score will improve.

Just as our golf game will improve if we adjust our swing, our lives will improve dramatically if we take an objective look at our lives.

Our self-importance is best understood when we examine God's love for us through Christ. If we base our self worth on God's grace, and grow in our understanding of grace in Jesus Christ, (2 Peter 3:18) we will have a secure and healthy self-worth based upon God's love, and not our position, bank account or our golf handicap. The result will be a growing knowledge of our true spiritual giftedness to strengthen and enjoy the body of Christ, and a growing desire to be involved in the lives of people who are searching for security.

Growing in grace will give us the security we so desperately seek. Then, we can use a 6-iron instead of a 7-iron, and be at peace with ourselves.

Dear God,
Help me to be realistic about my life. Help me
to not be proud, boastful or arrogant, but to
be humble in all things. May I always realize,
that my importance comes from Your love for me,
and not my own accomplishments.

PSALM 107:35

Eighteenth Hole

PAYNE STEWART'S PEACE

GOLF INSIGHT

"There used to be a void in my life ... The peace I have now is so wonderful. I don't understand how I lived so long without it."

Payne Stewart

GOD'S INSIGHT

"Therefore, since we have been justified through faith, we have peace with God through our Lord Jesus Christ, through whom we have gained access by faith into this grace in which we now stand."

Romans 5:1-2

GOLF & LIFE

An oil company executive who recently retired said, "I'm now playing golf six days a week and the unthinkable has happened ... I'm bored." The phrase, "Life's a game but golf is serious", is reality for many people. However, no matter how much you love golf, it cannot provide "the peace that passes understanding" to our souls!

We all have a void in our lives that only God can fill. Golf can't fill it. Money can't fill it. Success can't fill it. Family and friends can't fill it, even though they may try. Knowing God and His peace is the key to living a fulfilled life. Payne Stewart understood this, and because he understood it, he possessed a peace that passes understanding and a purpose for living. The good news is, that same peace is available to everyone who desires it. All we have to do is ask.

Dear Lord,
I want to know You. I want my life to have purpose and meaning beyond my earthly successes and accomplishments. There is a void in my life that only You can fill. I want to have a relationship with You, and in so doing, find peace and a purpose for living, as I share with others what I have found in You.

Ninteenth Hole

BEFORE IT'S TOO LATE

GOLF INSIGHT

"Pars are very good. Birdies are great. Eagles are spectacular. However, the most excellent thing a golfer can have is peace with God, and the ability to live out their faith in love."

Ted Sprague

GOD'S INSIGHT

"And now these three remain: faith, hope and love. But the greatest of these is love."

1 Corinthians 13:13

BEFORE IT'S TOO LATE

Golf and life have so many challenges
But when things are going well, O what a ride!
Hitting the white pellet where it is supposed to go
Creates an overwhelming sense of pride.

Life on the other hand, is filled with varied situations
Whether we're on the top or bottom.
That's why God has given us His precious promises
through winter, spring, summer and autumn.

Golf provides so many benefits it's hard to name them all.
Outdoors, relaxation, and of course people for whom He died.
However, we've missed a few short putts, sprayed a few drives,
And sometimes our character looks weak, as we have cried.

We need THE MASTER'S TOUCH in all of life today,
Before our life is interrupted by a sudden turn of fate.
We must live out our faith, hope and love,
By God's grace, before it's too late.

Ted Sprague resides in Marietta, Georgia with his wife Tudi. They have two daughters and three grandchildren. In addition to being an avid golfer, Sprague has served as the executive director for the Georgia Golf Hall of Fame, marketing director for the Jack Nicklaus Museum, and marketing consultant for the World Golf Village in St. Augustine, Florida.

For 25 years of his career, he has been involved in the destination marketing industry, serving as president of the Atlanta Convention & Visitors Bureau from 1982-1991. Since then he has been the principal

of two consulting firms, Travel Destinations and Sprague and Associates, serving over 60 cities, attractions, and destinations. He has also worked with Promise Keepers, Haggai Institute, and Fellowship of Companies for Christ, serving as a facilitator of CEO's on a monthly basis. He is currently consulting as executive director for the New York City Vision, for The King's College in the Empire State Building and for World2One.com.

Since becoming a Christian, Ted has had the privilege of speaking to groups in more than 200 cities, 40 states, and several countries sharing the gospel of Jesus Christ.

Larry Dyke, recognized as America's Golf Artist, is one of the most successful and acclaimed artists of his generation.

Within a year of his first golf print release, Larry Dyke became the nation's most collected golf artist. His paintings reflect a realism and precise accuracy rarely found in golf art, but perhaps their strongest appeal is that each one offers every golfer's dream: to have a world-class course all to himself—under perfect conditions—on a perfect day. He succeeds in making this happen, by capturing the moment, and making it last forever.

Dyke is an artist who also loves to golf. He took up the sport at age thirteen, playing on public courses in and around his west Texas home of Borger. Today, he holds the unique spot as the premiere artist for some of the world's most scenic course and vistas.

With respect to the similarities between the seemingly disparate disciplines of painting and golf, Dyke points out that both are "internal to some degree, and they require a good eye, and a keen dexterity too." And of course, they both require strokes.

Dyke's paintings of golf courses and his many powerful landscapes are inspired by his deep personal belief in Christ, and each reflects the glory of nature, the value of art, and his own personal call.

Larry and his family reside in Friendswood, Texas.

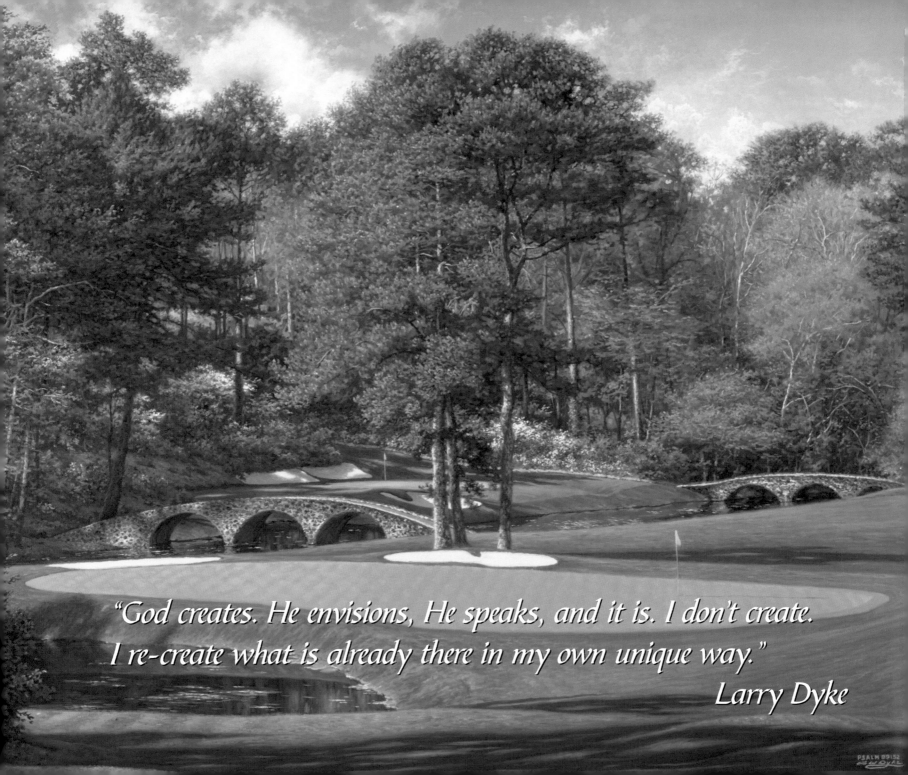

"*God creates. He envisions, He speaks, and it is. I don't create.
I re-create what is already there in my own unique way.*"

Larry Dyke